"Beer for Breakfast"

# The Chili Cookbook

One-Pot Family Worthy Recipes

BY

*Daniel Humphreys*

Copyright 2019 Daniel Humphreys

# License Notes

No part of this Book can be reproduced in any form or by any means including print, electronic, scanning or photocopying unless prior permission is granted by the author.

All ideas, suggestions and guidelines mentioned here are written for informative purposes. While the author has taken every possible step to ensure accuracy, all readers are advised to follow information at their own risk. The author cannot be held responsible for personal and/or commercial damages in case of misinterpreting and misunderstanding any part of this Book

# Table of Contents

Introduction .................................................................. 6

   Crock Pot Black Bean and Quinoa Chili ..................... 8

   Turkey and White Bean Chili ....................................... 12

   Sweet Potato and Chorizo Chili .................................. 15

   Chili Muffin Cups ........................................................ 17

   Slow Cooker Black Bean Taco Chili ........................... 20

   Vegetable Lime and Chickpea Chili ............................ 23

   Pumpkin and Black Bean Chili ................................... 26

   Butternut Squash Chili ................................................ 29

   Homemade White Chicken Chili ................................. 32

   Slow Cooker Pumpkin Beer Chili ................................ 35

   Picadillo Chili .............................................................. 38

Chile Cornbread Pie ........................................................ 41

Vegetarian Chili ............................................................. 45

Five Bean Chili .............................................................. 49

Baja Chicken Chili ......................................................... 52

Cowboy Chili ................................................................. 55

Cheese Tortellini Chili ................................................... 58

Football Beer Chili ........................................................ 61

Chili Mac and Cheese ................................................... 64

Barbecue Chicken Bean Chili ........................................ 67

Jalapeno Popper Turkey Chili ........................................ 70

Famous Crock Pot Chili ................................................ 73

Apricot Turkey Chili ...................................................... 75

Classic Beef Chili ......................................................... 78

Lean Turkey Chili .......................................................... 82

Conclusion ........................................................................ 85

Author's Afterthoughts ..................................................... 86

About the Author .............................................................. 87

# Introduction

Making chili has become more of a regular custom in America then making hamburgers or hosting family barbecues. Chili is a dish many families make in order to bring people together. It is such a popular dish to make in America, in fact it is a dish that has been argued over for well over a century. Ever since it was invented, people from across the country have been arguing about not only how to spell the word chili, but whether or not chili should even have beans in it.

Regardless, if you are an avid lover of chili, then you have certainly come to the right place. Inside of this book, we won't be bothering with arguing what types of chili are the best or whether or not you should add meat into it. Instead I will be focusing on teaching you how to make homemade chili correctly. I will do this by giving you access to over 25 chili recipes that have been passed down my family through generations. Every recipe is made with taste in mind and I guarantee even the pickiest of eaters in your home will love each one.

Let's stop wasting time and get to cooking some chili!

# Crock Pot Black Bean and Quinoa Chili

There is no other delicious and healthy chili recipe that is quite like this recipe. One bite and everyone in your home will become hooked.

**Makes:** 8 servings

**Total Prep Time:** 4 hours and 50 minutes

**Ingredients:**

- 1 red onion, chopped
- 4 cloves of garlic, minced
- 1 red bell pepper, chopped
- 1 cup of baby carrots, thinly sliced
- 4 cups of tomatoes, chopped
- 2, 15 ounce cans of black beans, drained
- 1 cup of dried brown lentils
- ½ cup of quinoa
- 6 cups of vegetable broth
- 1 Tbsp. of powdered coriander
- 1 Tbsp. of powdered cumin
- 1 Tbsp. of oregano
- 3 Tbsp. of powdered chili
- 1 Tbsp. of tomato paste
- 2 Tbsp. of extra virgin olive oil

**Ingredients for the topping:**

- 1 dollop of Greek yogurt
- Lemon juice
- Shredded cheddar cheese
- Tortilla chips
- Chopped cilantro

**Directions:**

1. In a Dutch oven set over medium heat, add in the olive oil. Add in the onion, minced garlic, chopped red bell pepper, sliced baby carrots, powdered coriander and powdered cumin. Stir well to mix. Cook for 5 minutes.

2. Add in the tomato paste, chopped tomatoes and oregano. Stir well to mix. Continue to cook for an additional 5 minutes.

3. Transfer into a crock pot.

4. Add the remaining ingredients. Stir to incorporate.

5. Cover and cook on the highest setting for 4 ½ hours or on the lowest setting for 8 hours.

6. Serve with a topping of Greek yogurt, lemon juice, shredded cheddar cheese, tortilla chips and chopped cilantro.

# Turkey and White Bean Chili

If you are new to the world of chili, then this is the perfect chili dish for you to make. Made with undertones of rosemary and hominy, this is perhaps one of the most delicious chili dishes you will get the chance to try.

**Makes:** 6 servings

**Total Prep Time:** 1 hour and 20 minutes

**Ingredients:**

- 3 Tbsp. of vegetable oil
- 3 cloves of garlic, minced
- 4 tsp. of rosemary leaves, chopped
- 1 tsp. of dried oregano
- Dash of salt and black pepper
- 5 cups of low sodium chicken broth
- 1, 15 ounce of white hominy, drained
- 1 white onion, chopped
- 1 to 2 serrano chiles, seeds removed and minced
- 1 ½ tsp. of powdered cumin
- ¼ tsp. of cayenne pepper
- 1 pound of ground turkey
- 1, 15.5 ounce cans of cannellini beans, drain
- 3 Tbsp. of cornmeal

**Directions:**

1. In a Dutch oven set over medium to high heat, add in the vegetable oil. Add in the onion. Cook for 8 minutes or until soft.

2. Add in the minced garlic, minced serrano chiles, chopped rosemary, powdered cumin, dried oregano and cayenne pepper. Stir well to mix. Cook for 2 minutes.

3. Season with a dash of salt.

4. Add in the ground turkey. Cook for 5 to 10 minutes or until cooked through.

5. Add in the low sodium chicken broth and hominy. Allow to come to a boil. Lower the heat to low. Cook for 25 minutes or until thick in consistency.

6. Add in the cornmeal. Cook for 15 minutes.

7. Season with a dash of salt.

8. Remove and serve immediately.

# Sweet Potato and Chorizo Chili

This is the perfect chili dish to prepare on a cold winter's night. Be sure to serve this chili with cornbread or crackers for the tastiest results.

**Makes:** 8 servings

**Total Prep Time:** 35 minutes

**Ingredients:**

- 1 onion, chopped
- 1 pound of bulk chorizo sausage
- 2 sweet potatoes, cut in cubes
- 2, 15.5 ounce cans of chili beans
- 1, 14.5 ounce can of roasted tomatoes with garlic
- 1 ½ cups of vegetable broth

**Directions:**

1. In a Dutch oven set over medium to high heat, add in the onion and chorizo sausage. Cook for 8 to 10 minutes or until cooked through.

2. Drain the excess grease

3. Add in the sweet potatoes, chili beans, can of roasted tomatoes and broth. Stir well to mix.

4. Allow to come to a boil. Lower the heat to low. Cook for 20 to 25 minutes or until the sweet potatoes are soft.

5. Remove from heat and serve.

# Chili Muffin Cups

Make these delicious muffin cups whenever you need something to take along with you on the way to work.

**Makes:** 8 servings

**Total Prep Time:** 35 minutes

**Ingredients:**

- ½ pound of lean ground beef
- 1, 15.5 ounce can of chili beans
- 1, 16.6 ounce can of flaky biscuits
- ½ cup of low fat cheddar cheese, shredded
- ½ cup of sour cream
- ¼ cup of green onions, thinly sliced

**Directions:**

1. Preheat the oven to 350 degrees.

2. In a skillet set over medium to high heat, add in the ground beef. Cook for 8 minutes or until cooked through. Drain the beef. Add in the chili beans. Stir well to mix.

3. Grease a muffin pan with cooking spray.

4. Peel each biscuit apart into halves. Flatten into a 4 inch circle. Press into the muffin cups to form a cup.

5. Filling with 2 tablespoons of the chili mix into each cup.

6. Place into the oven to bake for 10 to 12 minutes. Top off with ½ tablespoon of shredded cheese. Place back into the oven to bake for 1 minute or until melted.

7. Serve with a dollop of sour cream and garnish of green onions.

# Slow Cooker Black Bean Taco Chili

If you are in the mood for both tacos and chili, then this is the perfect chili dish for you. Since it is made in a slow cooker, there is practically no food prep needed from you.

**Makes:** 4 to 6 servings

**Total Prep Time:** 4 hours and 10 minutes

**Ingredients:**

- 1 ½ pound of chicken breasts, trimmed
- 1, 15 ounce can of corn, drained
- 1, 15 ounce can of black beans, drained
- 1, 15 ounce can of petite tomatoes, drained
- 1 cup of yellow onion, chopped
- 1 cup of green bell pepper
- 1 jalapeno, chopped
- 3 cloves of garlic, minced
- 2 tsp. of salt
- 1 tsp. of black pepper
- 1/8 to ¼ tsp. of crushed red pepper flakes
- 1 ½ tsp. of powdered chili
- ¼ tsp. of cayenne pepper
- 2 ½ to 3 cups of chicken broth
- Shredded Monterey jack cheese
- Tortilla chips
- Sour cream

**Directions:**

1. In a slow cooker, add in the chicken breasts, can of black beans, can of tomatoes, chopped yellow onion, chopped green bell pepper, jalapeno, minced garlic, crushed red pepper flakes, powdered chili, cayenne pepper and chicken broth.

2. Season with a dash of salt and black pepper.

3. Cover and cook on the highest setting for 4 hours.

4. Remove the chicken and shred finely. Add back into the slow cooker. Stir well to incorporate.

5. Serve with a topping of the shredded Monterey jack cheese, tortilla chips and sour cream.

# Vegetable Lime and Chickpea Chili

As far as chili dishes go, this is one of the lightest. This is perfect for those who are looking for something filling, but don't want to load up on calories in the process.

**Makes:** 6 to 8 servings

**Total Prep Time:** 30 minutes

**Ingredients:**

- 2 Tbsp. of extra virgin olive oil
- 1 ½ cups of white onion, chopped
- 1 ½ cups of zucchini, chopped
- 1 ½ cups of yellow squash, chopped
- 1 cup of miniature sweet peppers, chopped
- 1, 8 ounce pack of baby bella mushrooms, thinly sliced
- 2 Tbsp. of garlic, minced
- 2, 15 ounce cans of chickpeas, drained
- 1, 28 ounce can of tomatoes, chopped
- 2 cups of vegetable broth
- ½ cup of cilantro leaves, chopped
- 3 Tbsp. of lime juice
- 2 tsp. of powdered cumin
- 1 tsp. of powdered chili
- 1 tsp. of salt
- ½ tsp. of black pepper

**Directions:**

1. in a Dutch oven set over medium to high heat, add in the olive oil. Add in the white onion, chopped zucchini, chopped yellow squash, chopped miniature sweet peppers and baby bella mushrooms. Stir well to mix. Cook for 5 to 10 minutes or until soft.

2. Add in the minced garlic. Cook for an additional minute.

3. Add in the can of drained chickpeas, can of chopped tomatoes, vegetable broth, chopped cilantro, lime juice, powdered cumin and powdered chili. Stir well to mix. Season with a dash of salt and black pepper. Cook for 5 minutes or until piping hot.

4. Lower the heat to low. Cook for 5 minutes.

5. Remove and serve immediately.

# Pumpkin and Black Bean Chili

This is a healthy and delicious vegetarian chile recipe that can make a great alternative to regular homemade chili.

**Makes:** 4 servings

**Total Prep Time:** 40 minutes

**Ingredients:**

- 1 Tbsp. of extra virgin olive oil
- 1 onion, chopped
- 4 cloves of garlic, minced
- 1 cup of pureed pumpkin
- 1 cup of canned tomatoes, chopped
- 1 cup of vegetable stock
- 1, 15 ounce cans of black beans
- 1, 7.5 ounce can of garbanzo beans
- 1 Tbsp. of powdered cumin
- 2 Tbsp. of powdered chili
- Dash of salt and black pepper

**Directions:**

1. In a skillet set over medium to high heat, add in the olive oil, chopped onion and minced garlic. Stir well to mix. Cook for 5 minutes or until soft.

2. Add in the pureed pumpkin, canned chopped tomatoes, vegetable stock, can of black beans and can of garbanzo beans. Stir well to mix.

3. Add in half of powdered cumin and remaining powdered chili.

4. Allow to come to a boil. Lower the heat to low and cook for 20 minutes.

5. Remove. Serve with a garnish of chopped green onions.

# Butternut Squash Chili

This is a healthy and delicious chili recipe you can make whenever you have a craving for chili. Made with hearty beef and beans, this is a dish everyone will love.

**Makes:** 6 servings

**Total Prep Time:** 55 minutes

**Ingredients:**

- 1 Tbsp. of extra virgin olive oil
- 1 pound of lean ground beef
- ½ to ¼ pound of butternut squash, cut into cubes
- 1 green bell pepper, chopped
- 4 cloves of garlic, minced
- 1, 15 ounce of red kidney beans, rinsed
- ½, 7.5 ounce can of corn, drained
- 1, 28 ounce can of tomatoes
- 2 cups of water
- 1 Tbsp. of powdered chili
- 1 Tbsp. of cumin
- 1 tsp. of white sugar
- Dash of salt

**Ingredients for the garnish:**

- Grated cheddar cheese
- Green onions, chopped
- Greek yogurt

**Directions:**

1. In a skillet set over medium to high heat, add in the olive oil. Add in the ground beef. Cook for 8 to 10 minutes or until browned. Drain the excess grease.

2. In the same skillet, add in the butternut squash cubes, chopped green bell pepper, minced garlic, can of beans, can of corn and tomatoes. Stir well to mix.

3. Add in 1 tablespoon of powdered chili, powdered cumin, 1 teaspoon of sugar and a dash of salt. Stir well to incorporate.

4. Allow to come to a boil. Lower the heat to low. Cook for 20 to 25 minutes or until the squash is soft. Season with another dash of salt.

5. Serve with a topping of grated cheddar cheese, chopped green onions and the Greek yogurt.

# Homemade White Chicken Chili

This is a delicious chili dish you can make whenever you are in a hurry to get dinner on the table. It is so easy to make, you will be able to make it in 30 minutes or less.

**Makes:** 8 servings

**Total Prep Time:** 30 minutes

**Ingredients:**

- 3 Tbsp. of extra virgin olive oil
- 3 cups of Vidalia onion, peeled and chopped
- 1 jalapeno pepper, chopped
- 7 to 8 ounces of canned green chiles, undrained
- 4 cloves of garlic, peeled and minced
- 4 cups of low sodium chicken broth
- 4 cups of cooked chicken, shredded
- 2, 15 ounce cans of cannellini beans, drained
- 1 Tbsp. of lime juice
- 1 Tbsp. of powdered cumin
- 1 tsp. of dried oregano
- Dash of salt and black pepper
- ½ tsp. of crushed red pepper flakes
- ¼ tsp. of cayenne pepper
- 1/3 cup of cilantro leaves, minced
- Tortilla chip strips, for serving
- Shredded cheddar cheese, for serving
- Sour cream, for serving

**Directions:**

1. In a Dutch oven set over medium to high heat, add in the olive oil. Add in the chopped Vidalia onion, can of green chiles and chopped jalapeno pepper. Stir well to mix. Cook for 8 minutes or until soft.

2. Add in the minced garlic. Cook for an additional minute.

3. Add in the low sodium chicken broth, shredded chicken, can of cannellini beans, lime juice, powdered cumin, oregano, crushed red pepper flakes and cayenne pepper. Season with a dash of salt and black pepper.

4. in a food processor, add in 1 cup of the cannellini beans and a splash of chicken broth. Blend on the highest setting until smooth in consistency. Pour into the Dutch oven and stir well to incorporate.

5. Allow to come to a boil. Cook for 8 to 10 minutes. Add in the chopped cilantro and cook for an additional minute.

6. Remove from heat.

7. Serve with a garnish of the tortilla chip strips, shredded cheddar cheese and sour cream.

# Slow Cooker Pumpkin Beer Chili

This is comfort food at its absolute best. It is an easy chili dish that is packed with so much flavor, you are going to want to make it as often as possible.

**Makes:** 6 to 8 servings

**Total Prep Time:** 4 hours and 20 minutes

**Ingredients:**

- ¾ pound of ground beef
- ½ cup of yellow onion, chopped
- ½ cup of green bell pepper, chopped
- 2 cloves of garlic, minced
- 1, 7 ounce can of corn, drained
- 1, 15 ounce can of black beans, drained
- 1, 15 ounce can of kidney beans
- 1, 14.5 ounce can of petite tomatoes, chopped
- Dash of salt and black pepper
- 1 cup of pureed pumpkin
- ¼ tsp. of powdered nutmeg
- 1/8 tsp. of powdered allspice
- Dash of ground cloves
- 8 ounces of pumpkin beer

**Directions:**

1. In a skillet set over medium to high heat, add in the ground beef. Season with a dash of salt and black pepper. Cook for 8 to 10 minutes or until browned. Drain the excess grease and transfer into a slow cooker.

2. In the slow cooker, add in the remaining ingredients. Stir well to mix.

3. Cover and cook on the highest setting for 4 hours.

4. Remove the cover and serve.

# Picadillo Chili

To kick things off, we have a delicious chili dish you can make whenever you are craving something a bit on the spicy side.

**Makes:** 4 servings

**Total Prep Time:** 30 minutes

**Ingredients:**

- 2 Tbsp. of extra virgin olive oil
- 1 onion, chopped
- 2 tsp. of powdered cumin
- 2 pound of lean ground beef
- 3 Tbsp. of red wine vinegar
- White rice, cooked
- Green olives, thinly sliced
- ½ cup of garlic, chopped
- 2 poblano chiles, seeds removed and chopped
- ½ tsp. of powdered cinnamon
- 1, 28 ounce can of tomatoes, peeled and chopped
- Dash of salt

**Directions:**

1. In a pot set over medium to high heat, add in the olive oil. Add in the chopped garlic, chopped onion and chopped poblano chiles. Stir well to mix. Cook for 5 minutes or until soft.

2. Add in the powdered cumin and powdered cinnamon. Cook for an additional minute.

3. Add in the lean ground beef. Season with a dash of salt. Cook for 8 to 10 minutes or until browned.

4. Add in the red wine vinegar and can of tomatoes with the juice. Season with a dash of salt. Allow to come to a boil. Lower the heat to low. Cook for 10 minutes or until thick in consistency.

5. Serve the chile over the cooked white rice.

# Chile Cornbread Pie

This is the perfect chile dish to make whenever you need to impress your friends and family with your chile cooking skill.

**Makes:** 8 servings

**Total Prep Time:** 1 hour and 5 minutes

**Ingredients for the filling:**

- 2 Tbsp. of safflower oil
- 2 carrots, chopped
- Dash of salt and black pepper
- 2 Tbsp. of tomato paste
- 1, 14.5 ounce can of tomatoes, peeled and chopped
- 1 onion, minced
- 4 cloves of garlic, minced
- 2 Tbsp. of powdered chili
- 2 pounds of lean ground beef
- 1, 15.5 ounce can of pinto beans, drained and rinsed

**Ingredients for the topping:**

- ¾ cup of all-purpose flour
- 1 Tbsp. of white sugar
- 1 ½ tsp. of baker's style baking powder
- 2 eggs, beaten
- ¾ cup of yellow cornmeal
- 1 ½ tsp. of salt
- 1 cup of buttermilk
- 2 Tbsp. of butter, melted

**Directions:**

1. Preheat the oven to 400 degrees.

2. Prepare the filling. In a cast iron skillet set over high medium heat, add in the safflower oil. Add in the minced onion, chopped carrots and minced garlic. Season with a dash of salt. Cook for 5 minutes or until soft.

3. Add in the powdered chili and tomato paste. Stir well to mix. Continue to cook for an additional 30 seconds.

4. Add in the ground beef. Cook for 8 minutes or until browned.

5. Add in the can of tomatoes along with their juices and the can of pinto beans. Stir well to mix. Allow to come to a boil. Cook for 2 minutes. Remove from heat and set aside.

6. Prepare the topping. In a bowl, add in the all-purpose flour, cornmeal, dash of salt and baker's style baking powder Stir well to mix. Add in the buttermilk, beaten eggs and melted butter. Stir again until moist. Pour over the filling.

7. Place into the oven to bake for 20 minutes or until baked through.

8. Remove and set aside to rest for 20 minutes before serving.

# Vegetarian Chili

Just as the name implies, this is a delicious chili dish that is perfect to make for those vegetarian dieters in your household.

**Makes:** 5 servings

**Total Prep Time:** 2 hours and 30 minutes

**Ingredients:**

- 3 ancho chiles, rinsed
- 8 cloves of garlic, peeled
- 1/3 cup of extra virgin olive oil
- 5 stalks of celery, chopped
- 1 Tbsp. + 1 tsp. of salt
- 2, 28 ounce cans of tomatoes, chopped
- 2 pounds of sweet potatoes, cut into cubes
- 1, 15 ounce can of black eyed peas, drained
- 2 Tbsp. of cumin seeds
- 2 Tbsp. of chipotle chiles in adobo
- 1 fennel bulb, chopped
- 2 onions, chopped
- ½ cup of tomato paste
- ¾ cup of dried brown lentils
- 1, 15 ounce can of black beans, drained
- Cilantro leaves, chopped and for serving

**Directions:**

1. In a saucepan set over medium heat, add in 3 cups of water and allow to come to a boil.

2. In a skillet set over medium to high heat, add in the ancho chiles. Cook for 2 minutes or until dark. Transfer into a bowl. Pour the boiling water over the chiles. Set aside to rest for 30 minutes or until the chiles are soft.

3. In the same skillet, add in the cumin seeds. Cook for 30 seconds or until toasted. Transfer into a food processor. Pulse on the highest setting until ground.

4. Drain the chiles and set the soaking liquid aside for later use. Remove the seeds and stems from the chiles. Transfer into the clean food processor. Pulse until a thick paste forms.

5. In a pot set over medium to high heat, add in the olive oil. Add in the chopped sweet potatoes, canned chopped tomatoes, black eyed peas and dash of salt. Cook for 45 minutes or until golden.

6. Add in the powdered cumin and ancho chile paste. Add in the can of tomatoes paste and season with a dash of salt. Continue to cook for an additional 5 minutes.

7. Add in 5 cups of water, the dried brown lentils and chile soaking water. Increase the heat to high and allow to come to a boil. Lower the heat to low and cook for 30 minutes.

8. Add in the garlic and continue to cook for 30 minutes or until the potatoes are soft.

9. Remove from heat.

10. Serve with a garnish of chopped cilantro.

# Five Bean Chili

This is a healthy and vegetarian classic chili you can make any night of the week. It is the perfect dish to make to warm you up.

**Makes:** 6 servings

**Total Prep Time:** 30 minutes

**Ingredients:**

- 1 red bell pepper, chopped
- 1 onion, chopped
- 2 tsp. of garlic, minced
- 2 cups of vegetable broth
- 1, 8 ounce can of tomato sauce
- 1, 15 ounce can of black beans, drained
- 1, 15 ounce can of cannellini beans, drained
- 1, 15 ounce can of great northern beans, drained
- 1, 15 ounce can of pinto beans, drained
- 2 ½ tsp. of powdered cumin
- 1 tsp. of smoked paprika
- 1 tsp. of salt
- 1 tsp. of powdered garlic

**Directions:**

1. In a pot set over medium to high heat, add in the chopped red bell peppers and onions. Cook for 5 minutes or until soft.

2. Add in the minced garlic and cook for an additional minute.

3. Add in the vegetable broth, can of tomato sauce, can of black, cannellini, great northern and pinto beans. Stir well to evenly mix.

4. Allow to come to a boil.

5. Add in the powdered cumin, smoked paprika, dash of salt and powdered garlic. Stir well to incorporate.

6. Lower the heat to low. Cook for 15 to 20 minutes.

7. Remove and serve immediately.

# Baja Chicken Chili

This is a delicious chili recipe you can make whenever you want to try something new. Be sure to serve with cornbread or fresh bread for the tastiest results.

**Makes:** 12 servings

**Total Prep Time:** 50 minutes

**Ingredients:**

- 4 Tbsp. of vegetable oil, evenly divided
- 4 red bell peppers, chopped
- 2 green bell peppers, chopped
- 2 cups of onion, chopped
- 8 cloves of garlic, chopped
- 2 pounds of chicken breasts, boneless, skinless and cut into cubes
- 2 tsp. of powdered cumin
- Dash of black pepper
- ¼ tsp. of red pepper
- 3 Tbsp. of powdered chili
- 1, 32 ounce can of low sodium chicken broth
- 1, 28 ounce can of tomatoes, chopped
- 2, 15.25 ounce can of kidney beans
- 1, 15 ounce can of whole kernel corn, drained
- ½ cup of taco sauce

**Directions:**

1. In a Dutch oven set over medium to high heat, add in 2 tablespoons of vegetable oil. Add in the chopped red and green bell peppers, chopped onion and chopped garlic. Stir well to mix. Cook for 5 minutes or until soft. Transfer into a bowl.

2. In the same Dutch oven, add in 2 more tablespoons of vegetable oil. Add in the chicken cubes, powdered cumin and red pepper. Season with a dash of salt and black pepper. Cook for 8 to 10 minutes or until the chicken is browned.

3. Add in the remaining ingredients. Stir well to mix.

4. Allow to come to a boil. Lower the heat to low. Cook for 10 minutes. Season with a dash of salt.

5. Remove and serve immediately.

# Cowboy Chili

One bite of this chili and you will feel as if you are being teleported to the Southwest. It is perfect to make once the weather begins to turn colder.

**Makes:** 6 servings

**Total Prep Time:** 30 minutes

**Ingredients:**

- 2 pounds of lean ground beef
- 2 Tbsp. of extra virgin olive oil
- 1 onion, chopped
- 1 red bell pepper, chopped
- 1 clove of garlic, minced
- 3 tsp. of salt
- ½ tsp. of black pepper
- 2 cups of water
- 1, 28 ounce can of tomatoes, crushed
- 1, 14.5 ounce can of tomatoes, stewed
- 2, 15 ounce cans of kidney beans, drained
- 1/3 cup of powdered chili
- ½ tsp. of cayenne pepper
- 2 tsp. of powdered cumin

**Directions:**

1. In a pot set over medium to high heat, add in the olive oil and ground beef. Season with a dash of salt and black pepper. Cook for 8 to 10 minutes or until the beef is browned.

2. Add in the water, can of crushed tomatoes, can of stewed tomatoes, can of kidney beans, powdered chili, cayenne pepper and powdered cumin. Stir well to mix.

3. Allow to come to a boil. Lower the heat to low. Cook for 20 minutes.

4. Remove and serve immediately.

# Cheese Tortellini Chili

This is the perfect chili recipe to make if you are a huge Italian food lover! It is great to make whenever you are feeling a bit under the weather.

**Makes:** 4 servings

**Total Prep Time:** 4 hours and 10 minutes

**Ingredients:**

- 1 pound of lean ground beef
- 2 cups of cheese tortellini
- 2, 15 ounce cans of tomatoes, chopped
- 1, 15 ounce can of chili beans
- 2 cups of water
- 2 tsp. of powdered chili
- 1 tsp. of powdered garlic
- Dash of salt

**Directions:**

1. In a skillet set over medium to high heat, add in the ground beef. Cook for 8 to 10 minutes or until browned. Transfer into a slow cooker.

2. In the slow cooker, add in the can of chopped tomatoes, can of chili beans, water, powdered chili, powdered garlic and dash of salt. Stir well to mix.

3. Cover and cook on the lowest setting for 4 hours.

4. During the last hour of cooking, add in the cheese tortellini. Continue to cook for the remaining hour.

5. Remove the cover and serve immediately.

# Football Beer Chili

There is nothing that scream a tailgate party quite like homemade chili. This recipe is perfect to prepare during your next sporting event.

**Makes:** 6 servings

**Total Prep Time:** 8 hours and 35 minutes

**Ingredients:**

- 1 ½ pounds of lean ground beef
- 1 green bell pepper, chopped
- 1 white onion, chopped
- 2 cloves of garlic, minced
- 1, 28 ounce can of tomatoes, drained
- 3 Tbsp. of powdered chili
- 1 Tbsp. of Worcestershire sauce
- 1 Tbsp. of powdered cumin
- 1 Tbsp. of dried oregano
- 1 Tbsp. of salt
- 1 Tbsp. of tomato paste
- 1 bottle of ale
- 1, 15 ounce can of red kidney beans, drained
- 1, 15 ounce can of cannellini beans, drained
- Dash of black pepper

**Directions:**

1. In a skillet set over medium to high heat, add in the ground beef, chopped white onion and chopped green bell pepper. Stir well to mix. Cook for 10 minutes or until browned. Transfer into a slow cooker.

2. Add in the minced garlic. Continue to cook for an additional 1 to 2 minutes.

3. In a saucepan set over high heat, fill with 4 inches of water. Allow to come to a boil. Add in the drained tomatoes. Boil for 1 to 2 minutes or until the skins begin to peel. Remove from the pan. Peel the skin and remove the seeds. Crush and add into the slow cooker.

4. Add in the remaining ingredients.

5. Cover and cook on the lowest setting for 4 to 8 hours.

6. Remove the cover. Serve immediately.

# Chili Mac and Cheese

This is a chili dish that combines two of the ultimate comfort dish into one savory meal that everybody will fall in love with.

**Makes:** 4 servings

**Total Prep Time:** 30 minutes

**Ingredients:**

- 1 Tbsp. of extra virgin olive oil
- 2 cloves of garlic, minced
- 1 onion, chopped
- 8 ounces of lean ground beef
- 4 cups of chicken broth
- 1, 14.5 ounce can of tomatoes, chopped
- ¾ cup of white kidney beans, canned and drained
- ¾ cup of red kidney beans, canned and drained
- 2 tsp. of powdered chili
- 1 ½ tsp. of powdered cumin
- Dash of salt and black pepper
- 10 ounces of elbow pasta
- ¾ cup of shredded cheddar cheese
- 2 Tbsp. of parsley leaves, chopped

**Directions:**

1. In a Dutch oven set over medium to high heat, add in the olive oil. Add in the minced garlic, chopped onion and ground beef. Stir well to mix and cook for 5 minutes. Drain the excess fat.

2. Add in the chicken broth, chopped tomatoes, canned white beans, canned red kidney beans, powdered chili and powdered cumin. Stir well to mix. Season with a dash of salt and black pepper.

3. Allow to come to a boil. Lower the heat to low. Cook for 15 minutes or until the pasta is soft.

4. Remove from heat.

5. Top off with the shredded cheddar cheese. Cover and cook for an additional 2 minutes or until melted.

6. Garnish with chopped parsley. Serve immediately.

# Barbecue Chicken Bean Chili

This is a protein packed chili dish that is perfect for those who are looking to gain muscle. Best of all it is packed with a delicious barbecue flavor that is hard to resist.

**Makes:** 10 servings

**Total Prep Time:** 20 minutes

**Ingredients:**

- 1 Tbsp. of vegetable oil
- 20 ounces of chicken breasts, boneless, skinless and cut into cubes
- ½ cup of hickory barbecue sauce
- 1, 15.5 ounce can of garbanzo beans
- 1, 15.25 ounce can of kidney beans
- 1, 15 ounce can of black beans
- 2, 14.5 ounce cans of tomatoes with green chiles, chopped
- 1 cup of mild salsa

**Directions:**

1. In a Dutch oven set over medium to high heat, add in the olive oil. Add in the chicken breasts. Cook for 8 to 10 minutes or until cooked through.

2. Add in the barbecue sauce. Stir well until the chicken is coated.

3. Add in the remaining ingredients. Stir well to incorporate.

4. Allow to come to a boil. Lower the heat to low. Cover and cook for 10 minutes.

5. Remove and serve immediately.

# Jalapeno Popper Turkey Chili

This is a delicious chili dish you can make whenever you are craving something on the spicy side. It is perfect to make during the weekend.

**Makes:** 6 servings

**Total Prep Time:** 50 minutes

**Ingredients:**

- 2 Tbsp. of EVOO
- 1 red onion, chopped
- 2 jalapenos, seeds removed and chopped
- 3 cloves of garlic, minced
- 1 pound of lean ground turkey
- 2 Tbsp. of taco seasoning
- 1, 15 ounce of black beans, drained
- 1, 15 ounce of corn, drained
- 1, 15 ounce can of fire roasted tomatoes
- ½ cup of mild salsa
- 1, 32 ounce can of chicken broth
- ½ cup of cilantro, chopped
- 4 ounces of cream cheese, cut into cubes
- Shredded Mexican style cheese, for topping

**Directions:**

1. In a pot set over medium to high heat, add in the EVOO. Add in the chopped onion, chopped jalapenos and minced garlic. Cook for 5 minutes or until soft.

2. Add in the lean ground turkey. Cook for 8 to 10 minutes or until browned.

3. Add in the taco seasoning. Cook for an additional minute.

4. Add in the cans of black beans, corn and tomatoes. Add in the mild salsa, chicken broth and chopped cilantro. Stir well to evenly mix.

5. Lower the heat to low and cook for 30 minutes.

6. Add in the cream cheese. Cook for 1 to 2 minutes or until melted.

7. Remove and serve with a garnish of the shredded Mexican cheese.

# Famous Crock Pot Chili

This is a chili dish that has won several awards at local and nationwide state fairs. It is the perfect chili to make whenever you want to spoil your friends and family.

**Makes:** 16 servings

**Total Prep Time:** 8 hours and 20 minutes

**Ingredients:**

- 3 pounds of ground beef, cooked
- 2, 14.5 ounce cans of petite tomatoes, chopped
- 1 onion, chopped
- 1, 30 ounce can of tomato sauce
- 1, 15.5 ounce can of chili beans
- 2 cups of water
- 2 Tbsp. of powdered chili
- 1 ½ tsp. of garlic salt
- 4 tsp. of powdered cumin
- 2 tsp. of dried oregano

**Directions:**

1. In a slow cooker, add in all of the ingredients. Stir well to mix.

2. Cover and cook on the lowest setting for 8 to 10 hours.

3. Remove the cover. Serve with a topping of shredded cheddar cheese.

# Apricot Turkey Chili

This is a delicious chili dish that is perfect to make whenever you have a sweet tooth that needs to be satisfied.

**Makes:** 4 servings

**Total Prep Time:** 20 minutes

**Ingredients:**

- 1 tsp. of vegetable oil
- 20 ounces of lean ground beef
- 1 onion, chopped
- 2 cloves of garlic, chopped
- 1 Tbsp. of powdered chili
- 2 tsp. of dried oregano
- 1 tsp. of powdered cumin
- ½ tsp. of salt
- 1 Tbsp. of honey
- 1 tsp. of hot sauce
- 2 cups of low sodium beef broth
- 1, 15 ounce can of black beans, drained
- 1/3 cup of raisins
- 1/3 cup of dried apricots, chopped
- 1/3 cup of ketchup

**Directions:**

1. In a skillet set over medium to high heat, add in the vegetable oil. Add in the ground beef, chopped onion, chopped garlic, powdered chili, dried oregano and powdered cumin. Season with a dash of salt. Stir well to mix. Cook for 8 to 10 minutes or until the turkey is browned.

2. Add in the remaining ingredients. Stir well to incorporate.

3. Allow to come to a boil. Lower the heat to low. Cook for 10 minutes or until the apricots are soft.

4. Remove from heat and serve immediately.

# Classic Beef Chili

There is no other chili dish that is as classic as this one. This is a chili recipe you can alter with your favorite ingredients to make it even more delicious.

**Makes:** 10 servings

**Total Prep Time:** 3 hours and 30 minutes

**Ingredients:**

- 4 ½ cups + 5 cups of water
- 4 dried guajillo chiles
- 1 dried chipotle chile
- 1, 28 ounce of tomatoes, whole and peeled
- ½ tsp. of dried oregano
- 1 tsp. of white vinegar
- 4 pounds of beef sirloin, cut into cubes
- 2, 15.5 ounce cans of kidney beans, drained
- 4 dried ancho chiles
- 4 dried mulato chiles
- 8 cloves of garlic
- ¼ tsp. of powdered cumin
- Dash of salt and black pepper
- 5 Tbsp. of extra virgin olive oil, evenly divided
- 2 cups of onion, chopped
- Sour cream, for serving
- Shredded cheddar cheese, for serving

**Directions:**

1. In a saucepan set over medium to high heat, add in 4 ½ cups of water to a boil.

2. Preheat the oven to 300 degrees.

3. On a baking sheet, add the ancho, dried chipotle, dried mulato and dried guajillo chiles. Place into the oven to bake for 8 minutes or until soft. Remove and set aside to cool.

4. Once cooled, remove the stems and seeds from the chiles. Place into the pan of boiling water. Remove immediately from heat. Set aside to rest for 30 minutes. Drain the water, making sure to reserve 1 cup of it. Transfer the chiles into a blender. Blend on the highest setting until pureed.

5. In the blender, add in the tomatoes with the juice, reserved chili cooking water and 5 cups of water. Blend on the highest setting until smooth in consistency.

6. In a Dutch oven set over medium to high heat, add in 1 ½ tablespoons of the olive oil. Add in the beef. Season with a dash of salt and black pepper. Cook for 8 to 10 minutes or until browned. Transfer onto a plate.

7. In the same Dutch oven, add in the onions. Cook for 5 minutes or until soft. Add in the garlic paste and continue to cook for 2 minutes.

8. Add in the cooked beef and pureed chili pepper mix. Season with a dash of salt and black pepper.

9. Cover and cook for 2 ½ hours or until thick in consistency.

10. Add in the kidney beans and continue to cook for 2 minutes or until piping hot.

11. Remove from heat.

12. Serve with a topping of sour cream, shredded cheese and the jalapenos.

# Lean Turkey Chili

This is a lean chili dish you can make whenever you need to go light on the calories. It is great for people on a diet or who want to begin eating something on the healthy side.

**Makes:** 6 to 8 servings

**Total Prep Time:** 55 minutes

**Ingredients:**

- 3 ounces of ancho chiles, patted dry
- ½ of a white onion, cut into pieces
- 1 ½ cups of low sodium chicken broth
- 1 tsp. of dried oregano
- ¼ cup of safflower oil
- 2 pounds of turkey meat
- 1, 15.5 ounce can of pink beans, drained
- 2 cups of fire roasted tomatoes, whole
- 3 cloves of garlic, smashed
- ½ tsp. of powdered cinnamon
- 1 tsp. of powdered cumin
- Dash of salt and black pepper
- ¾ pound of smoked turkey necks, bones removed, cooked and shredded
- Sour cream, for serving
- Chopped cilantro, for serving

**Directions:**

1. Remove the stems and seeds from the ancho chiles. Place into a blender.

2. In the blender, add in the tomatoes, chopped onion, smashed garlic, ½ cup of the chicken broth, powdered cinnamon, dried oregano, powdered cumin and 2 tablespoons of the safflower oil. Season with a dash of salt. Blend on the highest setting until smooth in consistency. Transfer into a saucepan set over medium to high heat.

3. Cook for 20 minutes or until dark in color.

4. In a separate pot set over medium to high heat, add 2 tablespoons of safflower oil. Add in the turkey. Season with a dash of salt and black pepper. Cook for 8 to 10 minutes or until browned.

5. In the pot, add in the tomato mix, can of pink beans and 1 cup of the remaining chicken broth. Continue to cook for 5 minutes or until thick in consistency.

6. Season with a dash of salt and black pepper.

7. Serve with a topping of sour cream and chopped cilantro.

# Conclusion

Well, there you have it!

Hopefully by the end of this book you have found plenty of chili recipes you can make from the comfort of your own home. It is my hope that by the end of this book, not only do you have plenty of chili recipes you can prepare during those cold winter nights but feel encouraged to make new chili dishes you have never tried before.

So, what is next for you?

The next step for you to take is to begin making all of these delicious chili recipes for yourself. Once you have done that, it will be time for you to try to make your very own unique chili recipe completely from scratch.

Good luck!

# Author's Afterthoughts

*Thanks ever so much to each of my cherished readers for investing the time to read this book!*

*I know you could have picked from many other books but you chose this one. So a big thanks for downloading this book and reading all the way to the end.*

*If you enjoyed this book or received value from it, I'd like to ask you for a favor. Please take a few minutes to post an honest and heartfelt review on Amazon.com. Your support does make a difference and helps to benefit other people.*

*Thanks!*

**Daniel Humphreys**

# About the Author

***Daniel Humphreys***

Many people will ask me if I am German or Norman, and my answer is that I am 100% unique! Joking aside, I owe my cooking influence mainly to my mother who was British! I can certainly make a mean Sheppard's pie, but when it comes to preparing Bratwurst sausages and drinking beer with friends, I am also all in!

I am taking you on this culinary journey with me and hope you can appreciate my diversified background. In my 15 years career as a chef, I never had a dish returned to me by one of clients, so that should say something about me!

Actually, I will take that back. My worst critic is my four years old son, who refuses to taste anything that is green color. That shall pass, I am sure.

My hope is to help my children discover the joy of cooking and sharing their creations with their loved ones, like I did all my life. When you develop a passion for cooking and my suspicious is that you have one as well, it usually sticks for life. The best advice I can give anyone as a professional chef is invest. Invest your time, your heart in each meal you are creating. Invest also a little money in good cooking hardware and quality ingredients. But most of all enjoy every meal you prepare with YOUR friends and family!

Made in the USA
San Bernardino, CA
08 February 2019